Gardens
of
New England

PHOTOGRAPHY BY

Michael Hubley

NARRATIVE BY

David Epstein

First published in the United States of
America by:

Twin Lights Publishers, Inc.
8 Hale Street
Rockport, Massachusetts 01966
Telephone: (978) 546-7398
http://www.twinlightspub.com

ISBN: 1-885435-81-9
ISBN: 978-1-885435-81-1

10 9 8 7 6 5 4 3 2 1

The Mount *(opposite)*
LENOX, MASSACHUSETTS

(frontispiece)
RESIDENTIAL GARDEN, MAINE

(jacket front)
FULLER GARDENS

(jacket back)
GLEN MAGNA FARMS

Book design by:
SYP Design & Production, Inc.
www.sypdesign.com

Printed in China

Nothing Gold Can Stay

Nature's first green is gold,
Her hardest hue to hold.
Her early leaf's a flower;
But only so an hour.
Then leaf subsides to leaf,
So Eden sank to grief,
So dawn goes down to day
Nothing gold can stay.

—Robert Frost

I remember as a young boy growing up in Portland, Maine, taking a path through the woods to my grandmother's house. The walk took just fifteen minutes, but it always felt longer. Along the way, I would see raspberries, ferns, and wildflowers. I would stop at a small pond before traversing the rest of the way under the dense shade of majestic oak trees. To me, this world was magical. All this life! All these colors! All these sounds! Finally, I would run through a local farmer's vegetable garden and into Nana's back gate. The first flowers whose names I learned were the beautiful purple bearded iris behind my grandmother's house. They brought me much happiness.

I began my own gardening career at age 10, when my grandfather gave me some tomato seeds to grow. Now, vegetables have been a part of my summers for nearly 35 years. For my college essay, I chose to write about gardening. Now, as a meteorologist and landscape designer, it gives me great pleasure to offer gardening tips on WCVB-TV in Boston. I also created and host the website, GrowingWisdom.com, to help those who share my love of plants or have a desire to learn.

Gardening can teach some of life's most valuable lessons, including patience, nurturing, and selflessness. How many mornings, as a child, did I want to go play when the garden needed to be weeded? Gardeners learn to deal with the disappointment of a late frost, a drought or saturated ground.

Gardens of New England showcases some of the most beautiful gardens in the Northeast. Their colors, shapes, and textures reflect the diversity of our gardens as well as the passion and tenacity of our gardeners. Photographer Michael Hubley has that rare gift for capturing the "perfect garden moment," whether it's the exact second the sun's rays burst through a passing cloud, or the perfection of an open rose at its very peak. His eye for detail and mastery of the lens allow him to capture the tiniest droplet of dew on a leaflet, or to sense a fleeting breeze that will send ripples across a pond. His combination of patience and timing, and his quest to capture each subject in a different light or at a new angle, sets him and this collection apart from the ordinary.

I would be remiss not to give credit to Wayne Mezzit of Weston Nurseries, who spent hours sharing his wisdom and helping me to excel in the field. I also have been inspired by Gary Koller, whose wonderful designs I often emulate; and by Sheila Magullion, a lifelong gardener whose own passion continues to infuse my own. And finally, I am grateful for the collaboration of my editor, Karen T. Bartlett, who captured my passion for the garden and made my words flow like a summer brook.

Whether in need of inspiration for your own gardening space, a memory of your visit here, or for the simple pleasure of revisiting the spectacular blooms of summers past, let this book be your companion as you drink in the magic of the wonderful gardens of New England.

— Dave Epstein

New England Wild Flower Society's Garden In The Woods *(opposite)*
FRAMINGHAM, MASSACHUSETTS

Elizabeth Park

HARTFORD, CONNECTICUT

Designed in1894 by the famous firm of Olmsted and Sons for wealthy industrialist and statesman Charles Pond, Elizabeth Park encompasses more than 100 acres of gardens, paths and recreational spaces. Mr. Pond bequeathed the land to the city of Hartford with the stipulation that it be named for his wife, Elizabeth, and preserved as a horticultural park.

It's easy to forget, while gathered around this gazebo with loved ones for a wedding or other special occasion, that this pristine setting is just three miles from downtown Hartford. The structure creates a cozy spot for a special moment, leaving the rest of the world to go on unnoticed.

Passion For Purple

HARTFORD, CONNECTICUT

Deep purple clematis softens the base of this trellis, creating
the illusion of shrubs at the base of a tree. The columns seem
planted in the natural floor of red clay. The simplicity of colors
feels restful. The open belvedere is an enticing place to read a
book after a long day of work.

Royal Pathways

HARTFORD, CONNECTICUT

The arbor is a traditional way to create an inviting entrance to
a garden, as well as to support climbing blooms. In the regal
rose gardens at Elizabeth Park, summer sunshine provides the
nurturing that brings forth bold, beautiful colors and a sweet,
intoxicating scent.

Roses by the Hundred

HARTFORD, CONNECTICUT

More than 800 varieties of roses, from tea assortments to the highest of climbers, line many of the paths of the oldest municipally operated rose garden in the country. As one of 22 All America Test Gardens, Elizabeth Park tests some varieties of roses before they are introduced to the public.

A Unique Haven *(top)*
HARTFORD, CONNECTICUT

A lush covering of vines and other climbers brings this gazebo
to life. Temperatures inside can be 10 degrees cooler, creating an
oasis from the July heat, or a dry spot during a summer storm.

Captivating Passages *(bottom)*
HARTFORD, CONNECTICUT

Wildflowers hide this gazebo from full view, while beckoning
visiting bloom enthusiasts to follow the path of daylily, core-
opsis and helianthus toward the next stop on the garden tour.
Tours and workshops are offered by Friends of Elizabeth Park.

Nature's Artwork

HARTFORD, CONNECTICUT

It's obvious what the designers wanted to be the center of attention in this garden. The tree in the center is treated as a natural
sculpture, surrounded by the floral bounty of nature. Celosia,
ornament peppers, sunflowers and even the white flowers of
the bottlebrush buckeye (*Aesculus parviflora*) seem to be saying,
"Look over here! Isn't this special!"

11

Wickham Park

MANCHESTER, CONNECTICUT

Although it encompasses only eight of the 250 acres that make
up Wickham Park, the Oriental Garden is the largest of its spe-
cialty gardens. Among its loveliest features is the arched moon
bridge, which is typical of Japanese-style gardens. A spectacular
Japanese maple (*Acer palmatum*) graces the foreground.

ROSE
WALK

Paths Create Mystery

MANCHESTER, CONNECTICUT

Crushed stone and gravel often are used to create walkways.
This type of loose material encourages visitors at Wickham Park
to slow down and take time to appreciate the climbing roses as
they walk under the arches of the arbor. The curved path intro-
duces an element of mystery as to what might lie beyond.

Oriental Fountain *(top)*
MANCHESTER, CONNECTICUT

The influence of the Far East comes to life in the Lotus Garden at Wickham Park. The pagoda fountain stands tall, and creates intrigue for passing visitors. The traditional daylily plantings give it a woodland-like ambience.

Lighting the Way *(bottom)*
MANCHESTER, CONNECTICUT

Evening weddings and other events at the pagoda often are enhanced by the light from Japanese-style stone lanterns. The original lanterns would have been inset with small candles to provide just enough luminance to stroll comfortably through the garden at night.

Evil Spirits: Stay Away

MANCHESTER, CONNECTICUT

The Torri Gateway is based on a similar structure that the Wickhams saw during one of their trips to China. According to tradition, this type of gateway prevents evil spirits from entering the garden. The structure is painted a natural copper color to blend in with the copper highlights in the path.

Moon Gate *(above)*
BRISTOL, RHODE ISLAND

Civil engineer and self-taught garden designer John DeWolfe designed Moon Gate for Blithewold Mansion, Gardens & Arboretum. The stone archway is situated at the end of the Rose Garden, where a century-old chestnut rose dominates. A trellis encourages climbing flowers to encircle the opening. In full bloom, the flowers cover most of the stones.

Bamboo and Blue *(opposite)*
BRISTOL, RHODE ISLAND

Brilliant blue chairs amidst a Yellow Groove bamboo grove are among the many surprises one will encounter in the 33 acres of gardens at Blithewold. Bamboo makes a great hedge, and several types can be used in residential settings, although Yellow Groove bamboo is very invasive and not appropriate for a home garden. Some varieties can grow to heights of over 50 feet.

Living Rock

BRISTOL, RHODE ISLAND

One of the indications of a properly installed rock garden is
the illusion that the rocks are growing out of the ground. Here,
many small plants are perfectly situated along the stone path
and among the larger rocks. Blithewold is famous for its giant
sequoias, which stand in stark contrast to the tiny plants of the
rock garden.

Sloping Beauty

BRISTOL, RHODE ISLAND

The North Gardens at Blithewold slope gently toward Narragansett Bay. Several beds have been carved out of the grass, and made into perennial gardens. This breaks up the lawn, creating "rooms" on either side. Strategically placed chairs in front of one of these gardens illustrate how the garden serves as a wall against which furniture can be comfortably placed.

Everyone Loves Hydrangea

BRISTOL, RHODE ISLAND

For a garden by the seashore, hydrangeas are a must. These
flowering shrubs can bloom for months, providing color and
interest all summer and well into the fall. The Enclosed Garden
at Blithewold showcases several types of *Hydrangea macrophylla,*
including lacecap and mophead. Aluminum sulfate added to the
soil helps hydrangeas maintain their deep blue color.

Lotus Jewel

BRISTOL, RHODE ISLAND

Among the most ancient and revered flowers on the planet, the lotus (*Nelumbo nucifera*) has only two species. There are hundreds of hybrids, in the most spectacular colors and textures imaginable. These flowers are remarkable for their ability to shed water from their petals. Scientists study the lotus in order to mimic its properties in products and other applications.

Flowers for Cutting *(top)*
BRISTOL, RHODE ISLAND

A combination of annuals, perennials, and bulbs make up the cutting gardens at Blithewold. Annuals, the workhorses of the garden, respond well to being cut, forcing out new blooms all summer and extending the season into fall. Perennials and bulbs keep the garden fresh, as new blooms emerge throughout the season. Lollipop-shaped purple alliums are great in arrangements.

The Mansion *(bottom)*
BRISTOL, RHODE ISLAND

The branches of the Tupelo, or Black Gum tree, drape over the mansion at Blithewold, providing a welcome cooling effect on hot summer days. Shade trees can cool an area by up to 10 degrees. While the trees provide an anchor to the garden, the shrubs that border the home create a distinct setting apart from the lawn and flower gardens.

Sweet Climbing Color

BRISTOL, RHODE ISLAND

The fragrant sweet pea (*Lathyrus odoratus*) looks sensational as it climbs up a handmade bamboo fence. Sweet peas come in a variety of colors and can grow up to ten feet tall. They can be started from seed in the garden, and they love sunny spots. These beauties make super cut flowers.

Good Enough to Eat *(top)*
PORTSMOUTH, RHODE ISLAND

While dahlias aren't edible, the ones in the Green Animals
Topiary Garden, at the Preservation Society of Newport
County look good enough to eat. The blooms, as big as salad
plates, add striking color to a garden mix of vegetables, annuals,
and perennials. While the perennials neatly line the path, they
are left loose to give an informal feeling.

Perfect Pathways *(bottom)*
PORTSMOUTH, RHODE ISLAND

Common boxwood (*Buxus sempervirens*) has long been favored
by traditional landscape architects to give paths a formal style,
and the hedge at Green Animals is a perfect example. The brilliant color of the large castor bean bush (*Ricinus communis*)
brings the eye up and draws the observer toward the reeds that
lie ahead.

Sumptuous Plantings (*above*)

PORTSMOUTH, RHODE ISLAND

A potted flowering maple (*Abutilon*), and a riot of flowering tobacco (*Nicotiana sylvestris*), clinging vines, and enormous dahlias comprise this delicious section of the garden.

Purple Veil (*pages 26–27*)

PORTSMOUTH, RHODE ISLAND

A pole-mounted birdhouse surrounded by a purple profusion of verbena (*Verbena bonariensis*) make one of the most compelling gardens at Green Animals. Verbena is a perennial that botanists call a cyme: the flowers open first from the center. Its airy habit allows sunlight to pass through to other plantings. Deadheading (removing the spent blooms) encourages a bushier and fuller look.

Peaceable Green Kingdom (*top*)
PORTSMOUTH, RHODE ISLAND

If there was any doubt as to why Alice Brayton named her father's estate Green Animals, visitors need only step into this part of the garden. Here, the elephant, the bear, and the unicorn coexist peacefully with 18 other topiary creatures. Created of California privet, yew, and English boxwood, these topiaries are lifelike, but they don't bite.

Perfectly Coiffed (*bottom*)
PORTSMOUTH, RHODE ISLAND

The word topiary comes from the Latin for ornamental landscape garden. This historic pruning method is practiced all over the world, from French châteaux to Japanese parks. The Green Animals Topiary Garden is one of the oldest and most notable in the United States.

Elephant and Parterre

PORTSMOUTH, RHODE ISLAND

Several parterres, or ornamental arrangements of gardens and
paths, set the stage for the stately green animals to dominate the
scene. Mixed annuals provide splashes of color in the center of
the parterre, and a spiral topiary rises like a waterless fountain,
creating the illusion of movement and sound. Several paths
offer the wanderer a choice of direction.

29

Color, Texture, Form *(above)*

PORTSMOUTH, RHODE ISLAND

When designing a garden, many landscapers will recommend variations in color, texture, and form. At Green Animals, they have done exactly that. The tallest plants are set in the background and slope downward toward the groundcover below. This garden has an informal style, in which the plants are allowed to grow unabashedly in all directions.

Cutting Beauties *(bottom)*

PORTSMOUTH, RHODE ISLAND

Dahlias are among the best cutting flowers available. They can grow several feet during the summer, so it is a good idea to use stakes to prevent them from flopping over. Native to Mexico, dahlias are tubers that must be dug and stored in colder climates. Dahlias love a full day of sunshine and will drink a lot of water.

Into the Allee

PORTSMOUTH, RHODE ISLAND

Originated by the French for formal estates, the allee is a path
of tall trees leading to a point of interest, such as a statue or a
temple. Some allees were designed to give the illusion of infinity.
The stairs and path at Green Animals embody the essence of an
allee. The hydrangeas point to the stairs, and the openness
ahead takes the eye forward.

Elephant Ear Walls *(top)*
PROVIDENCE, RHODE ISLAND

A key goal in creating a garden is to maximize the allotted space. Instead of walls, the gardeners at Roger Williams Park Botanical Center have utilized large, dark elephant ear plants as a divider to separate two small gardens. Potted bromeliads give some nice color without demanding precious space.

Fun with Textures *(botom)*
PROVIDENCE, RHODE ISLAND

The day may be hot and humid, but the furry, fuzzy-looking chenille plant (*Acalypha hispida*) at Roger Williams Park looks like the perfect material for making a cozy sweater. The palm in the background, by contrast, is not so inviting to the touch.

Hidden Oasis

PROVIDENCE, RHODE ISLAND

Flanked by scores of tropical blooms, this water garden clearly stands out behind the pink anthuriums, also called flamingo flowers. These stems are popular in floral arrangements, and each variety has its own unique scent to attract a variety of birds, bees, and butterflies in their natural habitats.

Glass Jungle *(top)*
PROVIDENCE, RHODE ISLAND

Stepping into the 12,000 square-foot ecosystem of tropical trees, shrubs and flowering plants, one might feel transported to a Brazilian rainforest. Among the largest display greenhouses in New England, this exotic space at Roger Williams Park Botanical Center is infused with the sweet scent of jasmine. The only things missing are monkeys swinging from the trees.

Pretty In Pink *(botom)*
PROVIDENCE, RHODE ISLAND

Pink flamingo-like anthuriums are carefully matched with the ti plant (*Cordyline terminalis*) behind the fountain centerpiece at Roger Williams Park. Large tropical leaves provide focal points and give movement to the garden. In recent years, there has been a surge in the popularity of tropicals for home gardens. Designers use these plants to give a unique look to the grounds of traditional homes.

Prayer Plant

PROVIDENCE, RHODE ISLAND

The prayer plant (*Maranta leuconeura*) in the foreground thrives in bright light and high humidity. Its leaves close at night and reopen in the morning. Here in the greenhouse, the cold winter outside is not a problem. Inside the home, this plant likes a warm spot with some humidity. Misting the plant during the winter will help prevent the tips of the leaves from turning brown.

The Elms *(top)*

NEWPORT, RHODE ISLAND

The château at The Elms was fashioned in 1901 after the mid-18th century French château d'Asnieres (c.1750). The mansion overlooks well-manicured gardens featuring specimen trees and spectacular fountains. Designated a National Historic Landmark, The Elms was purchased by The Preservation Society of Newport County in 1962.

Canna, Contained *(bottom)*

NEWPORT, RHODE ISLAND

The tropical canna, given sufficient growing space in an oversize container, can make a bold statement on a large patio like the one at The Elms. When planting in containers, savvy gardeners use plants that cascade over the edges to blend the piece together and add height for balance.

Simple Symmetry

NEWPORT, RHODE ISLAND

The geometry of the home is reflected in the form of the garden. In deliberate artistry, the columnar shaped shrubs mimic the garden buildings and the arches within the stone wall. The geometric shapes of the lawn and parterre match the left and right wings of the mansion, bringing cohesion to the entire setting.

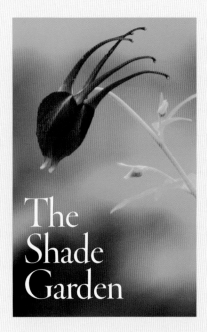

The Shade Garden

All plants require some light, so many homeowners find it a challenge to create a shade garden of diversity and beauty. Several gardens around New England have perfected the art of growing in the shade. Like plants, shade comes in a variety of forms, from the shadowy patterns beneath a honey locust tree to the dense shade within a stand of hemlocks. A garden can bask in brilliant sunshine for a few hours in the morning, and be enveloped in dappled shade in the afternoon.

Botanicals have adapted to this variety of light conditions. Many prefer the shade; others can be pushed to grow in greater than ideal amounts of shade; and some plants bridge the gap between light and dark, thriving in either condition.

Granny Bonnet
GARDEN IN THE WOODS

Native to North America and parts of Asia, the dainty granny bonnet, or columbine (*Aquilegia vulgaris*) is the state flower of Colorado. This late-spring bloomer loves sunshine and well-drained soil, and is a favorite of hummingbirds. If happy, it will continue to bloom throughout the summer. Besides pristine white, Granny bonnet blooms in a variety of blues, pinks, and blends.

It's All About the Leaves *(top)*
COLEUS. PRESCOTT PARK

The brilliant leaves, not the flowers, give the coleus its distinction. In fact, gardeners remove the flower spikes as soon as they appear, to keep the plant bushy and full. Coleus brings color to the shade garden. Shorter varieties make great border plants, while taller ones placed in the back of the garden offer dramatic flair.

A Woodland Carpet *(bottom)*
NATIVE GERANIUMS. GARDEN IN THE WOODS

The name *geranium* invokes images of the showy red, pink, and white annuals that New Englanders put out each Memorial Day, heralding the start of summer. However, native geraniums (*Geranium maculatum*) are mostly green and thrive in shady woodland settings. Native geraniums make a super ground cover.

Gardening with Coleus *(top and bottom)*

ELECTRIC COLORS, PRESCOTT PARK

The vibrant, bold, and bright-colored leaves of the coleus are great alternatives to blooms in areas where there are no flowering trees and shrubs. Its whirls of color create a wonderful pattern. Adding other plant varieties in similar colors will create a harmonious display, and a cohesive look to the garden.

Pretty in Pink

JAPANESE BLEEDING HEART. GLEN MAGNA FARMS

Aptly named for its resemblance to a broken heart, complete
with a drop of blood, the Japanese bleeding heart (*Dicentra
spectabilis*) might have grown in your grandmother's garden.
Like many other woodland flowers, the delicate blooms die
back to the ground in summer. If planted in a soil rich with
humus, they last a bit longer.

Ashintully *(above and opposite)*
TYRINGHAM, MASSACHUSETTS

Ashintully, Gaelic for "on the brow of the hill," is the name Massachusetts statesman and Egyptologist Robb De Peyster Tytus gave his 1,000-acre hillside estate in the early 20th century. Today, its spectacular collection of gardens showcases several unique habitats. From a beautiful stream to flower-filled meadows, it features both manicured and natural outdoor spaces.

The s-curved stone wall encircling the lawn, bright potted annuals and a misty fountain make this simplistic New England-style garden a restful place to relax with a favorite book, soak in the sunshine, and savor the sweet smell of summer.

Reaching Skyward

STOCKBRIDGE, MASSACHUSETTS

Four Doric columns, reminiscent of ancient Greece, are all
that remain of the original Georgian-style mansion, known
locally as "Marble Palace," which Mr. Tytus built on this site
in 1912. A raging fire destroyed the mansion in 1952.

Summer Perfection

STOCKBRIDGE, MASSACHUSETTS

Ashintully is maintained by The Trustees of Reservations, a non-profit conservation organization that maintains 83 public access properties throughout Massachusetts. A half-mile woodland loop trail takes visitors past the ruins of the mansion for breathtaking views of the Tyringham Valley below. The Regency Bridge and Trellis Triptych are two reasons why, in 1997, this garden received the H. Hollis Hunnewell Medal, which recognizes country gardens with rare and desirable ornamental plantings.

Newbury Perennial Gardens

NEWBURY, MASSACHUSETTS

Hyacinths float at the edge of this tranquil pond as water cascades over the falls in the background. It would be relatively easy to re-create this water feature at a private residence. Once established, water gardens need surprisingly minimal care and provide year-round interest. Plants and fish exist in harmony to balance the biological cycle of this self-contained ecosystem.

Smiling Susans *(top)*
NEWBURY, MASSACHUSETTS

Black-eyed Susan (*Rudbeckia hirta*) is among the most beloved endemic perennials in the country. This wildflower, honored as the state flower of Maryland, thrives in nearly any soil type and can handle sunshine from dawn to dusk. Pairing the black-eyed Susan with purples or even reds offers an interesting element to a stand of these hardy souls.

Welcoming White *(bottom)*
NEWBURY, MASSACHUSETTS

At Newbury Perennial Gardens, a trellis serves as a portal to another "room" in the garden. The white flowers of the hydrangea add balance and harmony to the whiteness of the trellis. Matching the color of an accent piece with the surrounding landscape helps blend the scene together in a uniform manner.

Calling All Butterflies

NEWBURY, MASSACHUSETTS

Butterflies flock to the Rose of Sharon (*Hibiscus syriacus*), which flowers in late summer. Here, they are in for a special treat, because they also find the brilliant Mexican sunflower (*Tithonia rotundiflora*), another New England favorite for attracting butterflies. Extremely heat and drought-tolerant, Mexican sunflower is most effective when planted where it can grow freely.

Conversation Starters *(top and bottom)*
NEWBURY, MASSACHUSETTS

Color excites. The heart beats faster. The eyes widen. Questions arise: "Is there fragrance?" "Is it native?" "Do you know the name?" Responses vary: "Wow that's bright." "I wish there were more." "I love it!" "It's gaudy." "Too much." "Look at that!" Whatever the thought, plants inspire us.

Berkshire Botanical Gardens *(top and bottom)*
STOCKBRIDGE, MASSACHUSETTS

An informal mix of plants gives the Artist's Shed a homey feel. Window boxes accent the walls and create the illusion that the plants are growing out of the entire structure. In springtime, the early-blooming *Primula japonica* creates a true primrose path. Primroses self-sow over time, creating a carpet of brilliant color.

Dave Epstein's Own Garden *(opposite)*
NATICK, MASSACHUSETTS

I stumbled upon this nameless rose at a nursery while shopping for other plants. The orange caught my eye, as something uncommon and a bit unusual. Pairing this with several clumps of Japanese blood grass (*Imperator cylindrical*), I have infused a section of the garden with warm summer tones. Through frequent clipping, the rose blooms several times each summer.

Stay for Lunch

NATICK, MASSACHUSETTS

Rather than use pea stone exclusively, I inset Pennsylvania garden path stones to provide a more stable footing. Friends and family may either come to the patio or cross a bridge onto the lawn. In the distance, a stone bench invites guests to relax and appreciate the space. Ironweed (*Veronia altissima*) stands over seven feet tall behind a conifer topiary.

A Bee's Best Friend *(top and bottom)*

NATICK, MASSACHUSETTS

"You have a lot of bees here," is a frequent comment from visitors to my garden. I have chosen plants that attract wildlife throughout much of my yard. Whether butterflies, bees, or birds, the relationship between flora and fauna is vital to a healthy ecosystem. Bees often begin pollinating autumn joy (*Sedum telephium*) in late August, without waiting for the flower to color up. In September, it is not unusual to see as many as 50 bees of various shapes and sizes on one clump of sedum. The black-eyed Susans in the background peak slightly ahead of the sedum. By pairing plants that flower in succession, the garden can bloom for weeks, or even months, without interruption.

Eye-Pleasing Color

NATICK, MASSACHUSETTS

The yard is like a painting. The plants, accents and hardscape
are the paint. Gardeners "paint" with color in subtle ways. I
blend the colors carefully so that when a flower blooms, like the
pink impatiens in the basket, it blends with something else in
the garden; in this case, the stone upon which the basket sits.

Smooth Transitions *(top and bottom)*

NATICK, MASSACHUSETTS

As a collector of plants, I primarily choose specimens that are native to the area. Sometimes, however, I find it interesting to add some exotics. My garnet-red Japanese blood grass (*Imperata cylindrica rubra*) shines brilliantly in the summer sun and provides a nice backdrop to the koi pond. It attracts few pests, making it an ideal plant. In autumn, it turns deep burgundy.

Boston Public Gardens *(top and bottom)*

BOSTON, MASSACHUSETTS

When warm weather awakens New England, throngs of people flood Boston Common and Public Gardens to enjoy the rebirth of another year. Opened in 1837 as the first public botanical garden in the United States, its ornamental design showcases the artistry of famed landscape architect Frederick Law Olmsted. Topiaries, flowering trees, and weeping willows give this spot a special feeling.

The flowering annuals along the walkways are replanted each season, and by early summer the roses tickle the nose with wonderful perfume. Several specimens of native and European trees join the weeping willows to create beautiful reflections in the pond. Monuments and sculptures give this garden in one of America's oldest cities an especially European flair.

The Swan Boats

BOSTON, MASSACHUSETTS

Spring has not officially arrived until the first swan boats are spotted on the lagoon at Boston Public Garden. The Paget family has been delighting young and old since 1877 with rides on their swans through the four shallow acres. Children can look for mallard ducks made famous in Robert McCloskey's 1941 picture book, *Make Way for Ducklings*.

Snowing Purple *(top)*
BOSTON, MASSACHUSETTS

Once every spring, for just a day or two, the flowers of the crabapples and cherries swirl to the ground as nature paints an artistic pattern with a blizzard of pink and purple petals. A few days later, the landscape will appear to passersby as though the storm never occurred.

Rite of Spring *(bottom)*
BOSTON, MASSACHUSETTS

The gentle rains of May cause the grass to go green almost overnight, and tulips burst open by the hundreds. The joy of witnessing the opening of bulbs planted the previous autumn never fails to awe. Massive areas of uniform colors create a bold statement: "Spring is here! Let all who are hungry from the long winter come and enjoy this annual feast."

Knee Deep in Tulips

BOSTON, MASSACHUSETTS

One great benefit of the Boston Public Garden's city location is the lack of deer. Tulips are among the deer's favorite treats, and it would not take long for a hungry pair of them to clip this area clean. Most tulips last only two or three seasons, so they are best used sparingly in the home garden.

The Mature Garden *(top and bottom)*

GLOUCESTER, MASSACHUSETTS

Echinacea, black-eyed Susans, daylilies, and assorted annuals
harmonize beautifully in Bobbie Brooks' residential garden.
Dense planting is one effective method to control weeds. The
sloping hillside is perfect for planting wildflowers and allowing
them to run wild. Several of the plants in this garden can be divided and moved to create other areas of color around the home.

Weeping Larches *(above)*

GLOUCESTER, MASSACHUSETTS

Weeping larches frame a Purple Martin birdhouse and mimic its upright form, creating a centerpiece in the garden. The gentle softness of these deciduous conifers begs to be touched, even petted. During autumn, the needles of this specimen will turn a warm yellow. In winter, snow will decorate its drooping branches, creating another season of interest in the garden.

Gentle Curves *(pages 62–63)*

GLOUCESTER, MASSACHUSETTS

The serpentine pattern of Bobbie Brooks' cutting garden at Distinctive Garden Design makes the lawn appear to snake its way gracefully around the beds. The curve adds depth to the scene, and frames each section of the garden. A trick to create an s-curve is to bend and re-bend a garden hose around the flower beds. The gardener can determine the perfect shape before starting to dig.

Hot Colors

WELLESLEY, MASSACHUSETTS

Hot oranges, yellows, and splashes of purple come together in Weezie's Garden for Children at the Massachusetts Horticultural Society's Elm Bank Horticultural Center. Large groupings of perennials allow each color to stand boldly on its own. The landscape artists slowly increased the height of the plantings, bringing the eye comfortably to the evergreen "frame."

Small Spaces, Big Color

WELLESLEY, MASSACHUSETTS

Container gardening continues to grow in popularity throughout New England. For those who have smaller spaces, or are just beginning to garden, containers offer an easily controlled space to learn. Here, potato vine and canna will thrive in the enclosed space. Even when canna is finished flowering, the colors of the foliage brighten the area.

Whirling Chairs *(top)*
WELLESLEY, MASSACHUSETTS

Weezie's Garden for Children at Elm Bank Horticultural Center
is a series of spiraling spaces filled with an abundance of plantings, with multiple points of interest along the way. The gardens
provide visitors a chance to truly get into the garden and be part
of the creation. The theme of movement throughout is exempli-
fied in these chairs with their spiraling pattern.

Hidden Spaces *(botom)*
WELLESLEY, MASSACHUSETTS

A walk through this garden reveals a group of scarlet poppies
in full bloom beside a water feature. Incorporating water into
a garden creates an instant focal point and gathering place.
Children are especially intrigued by water, where they can
search for fish, frogs, and other critters that may be hiding
under the lilies or behind a rock.

A Place to Learn

WELLESLEY, MASSACHUSETTS

The trial garden has been a staple of horticulture for centuries. At Elm Bank Horticultural Center's New England Trial Garden, growers can test newer cultivars of their specialized plants, such as roses and rhododendron, before the varieties become widely available. Some of the plantings used in this patio area may have been tested in the trial garden just a few years earlier.

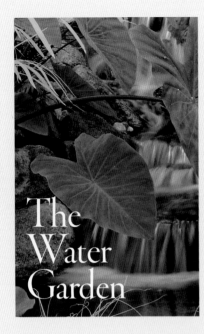

The Water Garden

From ancient temples to modern-day townhouses, the water garden has long been a part of civilization. It is no wonder that we humans are forever fascinated by that which makes up so much of our bodies. Water is the essence of life, and without it, life would cease to exist. Water carries with it many emotions such as fear, awe, tranquility, and humility. We yearn to be close to it, and today we carry it with us wherever we go.

A plant's relationship with water is equally as intimate. Although some plants can survive for long periods of time without water, they all need it. Certain plants evolve in such unique structures that they become one with the water. These plants not only survive; they thrive in this wet world.

Floating Leaves

BLITHEWOLD MANSION, GARDENS, AND ARBORETUM

Water serves as a linking element in this garden. The large leaves of the lotus float on, and soar above, the water. Its flower hovers in the air, connected to the pond by a thin stalk. Water hyacinths form a matted layer that responds with movement in the slightest breeze.

The Papyrus

ROGER WILLIAMS PARK BOTANICAL CENTER

One technique to provide interest to the water garden, especially when it is not in full bloom, is to vary the shapes of the plantings. Here, the long tendrils of the papyrus (*Cyperus papyrus*) fall gracefully toward the water below. Burgundy colocasia sits in the pond, and clumps of grass soften the lines of its stone border.

Whimsical Play

PRIVATE GARDEN, ROCKPORT, MASSACHUSETTS

Humor is an integral part of our lives, and the garden should be
no exception. There is an element of excitement when a gardener
finally finds that perfect statue, sculpture, or antique that puts
the finishing touch on a garden space. Here in Eileen Smith's
pond, the sounds of the garden are as important as the sights.

Easy as 1-2-3 *(top)*
BURDICK AND ASSOCIATES LANDSCAPE DESIGN

Gardening with water can be as simple as a bucket, some fish,
and a plant. It also can be an elaborate system of ponds, falls,
and streams, linked together and surrounded by rocks, stones,
and gravel. One can spend hours moving stones and plants to
create just the right look. Repositioning the rocks under a waterfall can dramatically alter the sound of the cascading water.

Monet's Muse *(bottom)*
PRIVATE GARDEN, ROCKPORT, MASSACHUSETTS

It is easy to see why the water lily (*Nymphaeaceae*) was the
subject of several of Claude Monet's works in the early 20th
century. Indeed, this bloom is truly a work of art. A native
of North America, the water lily can bloom throughout the
summer. It makes an easy and desirable addition to any
homemade water garden.

Afternoon Garden *(top and bottom)*

STOCKBRIDGE, MASSACHUSETTS

Naumkeag was the Choate family summer "cottage." The Afternoon Garden represents 30 years of collaboration between Mabel Choate and landscape architect Fletcher Steele. The gondola poles define the space, creating a "garden room" like those Mabel Choate admired in her travels. The low hedges suggest the idea of a carpet. The statue, entitled *Boy with Heron*, is by Frederick MacMonnies. Naumkeag is one of the properties overseen by The Trustees of Reservations.

Islands of Roses

STOCKBRIDGE, MASSACHUSETTS

In this view of the Naumkeag Rose Garden, several plantings of roses are set within the dry riverbed, which undulates lazily down the hill from above. The use of this type of pattern brings motion to the space. The pattern of the steps is repeated several times in the space, creating a cohesive feeling throughout.

Famous Blue Steps *(opposite)*
STOCKBRIDGE, MASSACHUSETTS

Anyone who has visited Naumkeag will recognize the famous Blue Steps. Sometimes called The Birch Walk in celebration of the paper birch (*Betula papyrifera*), it was designed by Fletcher Steele in 1938 for Mabel Choate so she could reach her cutting garden below. The stairs feel grounded by the paper birch, one of this region's most recognizable trees.

Philosopher's Stone *(above)*
STOCKBRIDGE, MASSACHUSETTS

Created by Fletcher Steele and Mabel Choate from an old cast iron grapevine-patterned veranda support, The Pagoda was designed as a focal point for the South Lawn at Naumkeag. Inside is a picturesque stone on a carved Chinese marble base that Miss Choate brought back from one of her trips to China.

Magic Seven

WESTFIELD, MASSACHUSETTS

The young Frank Stanley Beveridge loved gardening, and as an adult, he fulfilled a dream by building this park, now named Stanley Park. Mr. Beveridge favored the number seven, (count the letters in Stanley) which he considered magical. In building the tower, he used multiples of seven. He topped it with seven pillars. Beveridge died at age 77.

Symbols of Strength

An afternoon in Stanley Park offers something for everyone.
A certain oak tree in the park is said to be more than 200
years old. To Mr. Beveridge, its awesome presence symbolized
strength, endurance, and perseverance. The arboretum fountain
sits in front of a stand of ornamental trees: a testament to the
founder's commitment to nature.

Big Wheel

The big wheel of this working mill gets its power from the cascading waterfall in the background. A peek inside the building reveals many tools using this form of hydropower, and a walk over the bridge is rewarded with the sound of water as it splashes into the natural pond below.

Place of Many "I Do's" *(top)*
WESTFIELD, MASSACHUSETTS

Stanley Park's Rose Garden Fountain has been the scene of many weddings over the years. Roses have long been associated with this park, which is one of 20 test sites in the United States for new breeds of roses. Many varieties sold in garden stores today got their start right here in Westfield, Massachusetts.

Mix and Match *(bottom)*
WESTFIELD, MASSACHUSETTS

A walk through a public garden can bring a mix of emotions. Well-manicured lawns, perfectly clipped hedges, and fabulous blooms can make our own yards appear somewhat inferior. Containers offer an excellent way to bring great ideas from these gardens to our own spaces. Several containers of annuals light up a delightful corner of Stanley Park.

Flying Saucers *(top)*

FRAMINGHAM, MASSACHUSETTS

Elevated planters bring a modern touch to the woodland setting at New England Wild Flower Society's Garden in the Woods. One of several installations blending man-made artistic vision with the natural world, these playful UFOs by W. Gary Smith soar above the meadow below.

Kissed by Rain *(bottom)*

FRAMINGHAM, MASSACHUSETTS

Because each bloom may last just a few hours, the late spring/ early summer spiderwort (*Tradescantia hirsuticaulis*) appears most dazzling in masses. Each plant may produce more than 20 blossoms, which are edible. The spiderwort takes its name from the sticky sap in the stem which, when pulled, looks much like the silk of a spider's web.

Whirls and Swirls

FRAMINGHAM, MASSACHUSETTS

From the evenly spaced spines on a cactus, to the symmetry of a sunflower in bloom, patterns appear throughout nature. In the Yin-Yang Garden at New England Wild Flower Society's Art Goes Wild exhibit (2007), hay-scented ferns (*Dennstaedtia punctilobula*) swirl about white pine logs to form concentric circles, invoking a feeling of movement and life.

Fit to be Tied

FRAMINGHAM, MASSACHUSETTS

"Going green" is all the rage. At Garden in the Woods' Art Goes
Wild exhibit, (2007), prunings from the American beech (*Fagus
grandifolia*) create a dramatic colonnade next to the live plants.
This technique can be used to build a natural fence or a com-
posting bin. As the brush breaks down, it provides food for the
plants and shelter for animals.

Dazzling Shows *(top)*

FRAMINGHAM, MASSACHUSETTS

A walk on any path at Garden in the Woods is a sumptuous feast of eye candy no matter what season of the year. In springtime, visitors pause on the stone steps where an azalea shouts its full electrified bloom, before moving towards the next, yet unseen, floral treat.

Carefree Blue Star *(bottom)*

FRAMINGHAM, MASSACHUSETTS

While no plant is truly carefree, bluestar (*Amsonia tabernaemontana, A. rigida, A. hubrichtii*) comes close. These remarkable hardy plants continue to sparkle each year without any great care. Depending on the specific variety, the blue star can tolerate soil conditions from wet to sandy. Planted in masses, they present a great show.

Angel's Trumpets

The warm yellow blooms of angel's trumpets (*Brugmansia*)
reach heavenward in the Kinship Arbor at Tower Hill Botanic
Garden. Growers of this plant are a passionate bunch, finding
kinship in sharing cultivating techniques. This South American
native must be wintered indoors.

Pleasant Under Glass *(above)*

BOYLSTON, MASSACHUSETTS

Few are fortunate enough to have a greenhouse full of exotics in their backyards, so The Orangerie at Tower Hill Botanic Garden is a very popular place with garden enthusiasts. Most of the plants in The Orangerie are grown in containers, like these Versailles boxes, and are moved outside for the frost-free months.

A Thousand Words *(pages 86–87)*

BOYLSTON, MASSACHUSETTS

If a picture is worth a thousand words, this one speaks volumes. The azure sky is a perfect backdrop for this appealing meeting spot. The blooming yucca looks comfortable among the container gardens and the obelisk sculpture in the foreground. The lawn path divides the space, but allows for freedom of movement between them.

In the Beginning… *(top)*
BOYLSTON, MASSACHUSETTS

As if on cue, a heavenly rainbow appears at the Primordial
Fountain, where the plants are arranged according to the order
in which they appeared or evolved on Earth. The Primordial
Fountain, at the entrance to Tower Hill's Systematic Garden,
showcases the earliest plants: algae, mosses, liverworts, and ferns.

Loose and Fanciful *(bottom)*
BOYLSTON, MASSACHUSETTS

After a hectic and trying day, it is nice to come home to a cottage garden. Featured in Tower Hill's very first garden is the
Indian bean tree (*Catalpa bignonioides*). The beauty of this tree
can be most fully appreciated when used as a specimen on an
open lawn. Its tall panicles of white flowers appear in mid to
late summer.

Staircase of Stone

BOYLSTON, MASSACHUSETTS

A stroll through the Secret Garden, past airy grasses and lively daylilies, is sure to inspire gardeners with artistic ideas to take home. Stairs lead to double pergolas, which afford a panoramic view of the sunken garden from above. The bluestone theme, carried from the lower level up the stairs, binds it all together.

Private Bath (top)

BOYLSTON, MASSACHUSETTS

Just the right fountain, the perfect rock, a rare plant, or a charming birdbath can add a sense of wonder and excitement to a garden. The spiky tropicals at Tower Hill Botanic Garden create an exotic setting for feathered friends to come and clean their wings.

Neon Jungle (botom)

BOYLSTON, MASSACHUSETTS

One might expect colors like this in the jungles of Costa Rica, but the heat and humidity of a New England summer also are perfect for queen's tears (*Billbergia nutans*). These tropical beauties are started in the Orangerie, then brought outside each spring and strategically placed around the property.

Friends and Family

BOYLSTON, MASSACHUSETTS

The Kinship Arbor in the Systematic Garden is named for the closely related plant families, *solanaceae, polemoniaceae,* and *convolvulaceae.* While the plethora of plant material is as varied as the families from which they come, they are genetic cousins, each arising from the same class of plant.

Stop Here

LENOX, MASSACHUSETTS

A unique *objet d'art* is one way to compel visitors to pause in a garden. This latticework piece at The Mount was designed by Ogden Codman Jr., who also co-authored Wharton's first book, *The Decoration of Houses,* and designed much of the interior of the home.

First Real Home

LENOX, MASSACHUSETTS

Famed author Edith Wharton designed and built the estate that
she called her first real home, overlooking Laurel Lake in Lenox,
Massachusetts. Named The Mount, for her great-grandfather's
home, its every aspect reflects her influence. Wharton's niece,
Beatrix Ferrand, a founding member of the American Society
of Landscape Architects, designed the approach to the estate.

A Room With Views

LENOX, MASSACHUSETTS

A southwesterly stroll along the allee leads to the Italian
Garden. Its purposefully minimal planting, according to
Wharton herself, "has a charm independent of the seasons."
Fantastic views of the hills and lakes are framed by arched
openings on the garden's eastern edge.

Through the Lindens

LENOX, MASSACHUSETTS

An allee, or promenade, flanked by linden trees creates a lush lime-colored environment at the rear of the home. This promenade is an integral part of the three meticulously kept acres of formal gardens surrounding the mansion. Millions of dollars in donations and grants have returned this estate to a pinnacle of beauty. Wharton would be proud.

Carpet of Daisies

DANVERS, MASSACHUSETTS

A thick carpet of daisies sweeps its way through the vernal scene
at Glen Magna Farms, a property of Danvers Historical Society.
Peonies bloom prominently in the foreground. The lively color
palette, typical of early summer, lightens the border and creates
a natural transition to the ornamental trees and shrubs flowering
in the distance.

Dew-Kissed

DANVERS, MASSACHUSETTS

The peony is a must in any New England Garden. Even before
it opens, ants often flock to its sweet nectar. Once in bloom, the
peony infuses the air with sweet perfume. Some petal clusters
can reach over 10 inches across. When flowering is complete,
the graceful foliage of the peony stands tall all summer long.

97

Gather Together *(top)*
DANVERS, MASSACHUSETTS

The Glen Magna Farms estate, owned by Joseph Peabody in the mid 19th century, is now run by the Danvers Historical Society. Designed in the heyday of American gardens, its large frosty dahlias and the Russian-style summer house set a scene appropriate for the most formal or informal of gatherings.

Unfurled Beauty *(bottom)*
DANVERS, MASSACHUSETTS

There is a moment in time when a flower peaks. It may last but a few hours, or maybe a day. When gardeners wait in anticipation for such a moment, and then catch it, all the work becomes worthwhile. It is sad if they miss it, for they must wait an entire year to try again.

Hardy Rhododendron

DANVERS, MASSACHUSETTS

New England gardens endure six long months of harsh weather.
Finding a plant that can not only survive such challenging
conditions, but also thrive in them, is a formidable task. The
rhododendron is such a plant. Each spring, with vim and vigor,
it colors the countryside; and even when curled against winter's
cold, it remains green all year long.

Wisteria Wreath *(above)*
DANVERS, MASSACHUSETTS

Gluttonous wisteria flows atop the Romanesque columns at
Glen Magna Farms, creating a purple wig of petals in spring.
The thickness of the vines alongside the structure is a sign of
the maturity of these spectacular specimens. The open structure
allows full sunshine, resulting in an abundance of blooms.

Bold and Crisp *(opposite)*
DANVERS, MASSACHUSETTS

In contrast to the more loose and casual designs throughout
Glen Magna Farms, the lines here are clean and neat. The
circular water garden lets the eye wander in all directions. The
repeating pattern in each quadrant brings formality to the space,
while the weeping arbor in the distance lightens the mood.

Window to Eden

DANVERS, MASSACHUSETTS

Whether photographing a garden or designing one, it is important to establish a frame to set a scene. These pillars create a surreal look to the primordial soup of specimens in view. The design features a natural dirt path, which feels restful. One might imagine how the scene would change if brick or stone had been used instead.

Paths of Time

DANVERS, MASSACHUSETTS

The elegant walkway at Glen Magna Farms draws guests from the sundial to the water feature ahead, and then beyond to the terminal view. The design of the walk allows a choice of paths to take; each one allows a closer look at a special aspect of the garden.

Still Life *(top and opposite)*
BEVERLY, MASSACHUSETTS

Many subtle techniques come into play at Long Hill, which is overseen by the Trustees of Reservations. Wind and light play across the garden pond and constantly alter its appearance. The stillness of this pond is certain to be interrupted, as a toad contemplates his next leap. Boxwoods in each corner of a simple water feature (*opposite*) soften the harsh effect of the concrete.

Ostentatious Pair *(bottom)*
BEVERLY, MASSACHUSETTS

Native rhododendrons, coupled here with brilliant azaleas, create quite a spectacle. There is a bit of dissonance between the colors, which some will find artistically pleasing and others may consider too much of a clash. The wonderful thing about gardening is that there are few mistakes. If someone loves it, it's perfect.

Breathing Walls *(top)*

BEVERLY, MASSACHUSETTS

Each "room" in the landscape can serve a purpose. Here, the area is divided by a living wall. The passerby can see through the space. A garden party might spill over or remain contained; either way, the niche feels intimate and appropriate for the function.

Dressed in Green *(bottom)*

BEVERLY, MASSACHUSETTS

Hosta-lined paths, pots of annuals, and flowering trees beckon visitors to stop and admire the setting before embarking up the steps at Long Hill. Variegated ruffles of foliage ground the rod iron gateway, making it a part of the earth on which it stands.

Tunnel Vision

BEVERLY, MASSACHUSETTS

The illusion of dynamic flow captivates the imagination at Long Hill. As the viewer stands in one spot, the floral display appears to rush past. The perception of depth is accentuated by the strong linear design and the repetitive curve of the canopy.

Adaptation *(top and bottom)*
NORTHAMPTON, MASSACHUSETTS

Though we sometimes believe that plants exist for our viewing pleasure, plants evolve not for mankind, but to attract pollinators. This evolutionary process is celebrated throughout the plant world in such fine, intricate detail that it is easily overlooked. These stunning specimens are from the Lyman Conservatory in the Botanic Garden at Smith College.

Gathering Nectar *(opposite)*
NORTHAMPTON, MASSACHUSETTS

Bees and butterflies get the attention, but that tiny and wingless creature, the ant, deserves credit too. This six-legged insect has been crawling from flower to flower for 100 million years. Certain species of flora, usually low-growing plants with inconspicuous flowers, have evolved to take advantage of the ant's place in their miniscule world.

Botanic Garden at Smith College *(top and bottom)*

NORTHAMPTON, MASSACHUSETTS

Portions of the grounds at Smith College were designed by
Olmsted, Olmsted and Eliot whose founder, Frederick Law
Olmsted, Sr. is noted for the design of Boston's Emerald
Necklace and New York's Central Park. Thousands of plants
are under glass in the spectacular Lyman Conservatory at the
Botanic Garden, for students and the public to study and enjoy.

Lyman Conservatory

NORTHAMPTON, MASSACHUSETTS

At Smith College, visitors can get a break from winter's cold blanket when thousands of blooms scoff at the calendar and permeate the air with springtime fragrance. Hundreds of orchids and other botanical treats thrive in this world under glass, a tribute to the land where, a century ago, there were gardens, orchards, hayfields, and pastures.

English Style

NORTH ANDOVER, MASSACHUSETTS

A long path of lawn divides this English-style perennial bed. Foxgloves, iris, and peonies harmonize the scene. Cutting a path through the bed allows visitors to walk into the garden and become part of the picture, rather than just saunter up to it and observe. Stevens-Coolidge Place is run by The Trustees of Reservations,

Bearded Lady

NORTH ANDOVER, MASSACHUSETTS

This bearded iris (*Iris germanica*) is in perfect form, as its *standards* (petals that reach up) and *falls* (petals that fall down) capture the soft spring sunshine. Modern cultivars of iris bloom longer and in increasingly brilliant colors and patterns than ever before. Companion rose and iris plantings make the gardens particularly colorful and long lasting.

Synchronicity *(top and bottom)*

NORTH ANDOVER, MASSACHUSETTS

Perfect blooms deserve close scrutiny and admiration. For sheer romance in the sunken garden at Stevens-Coolidge Place, the gardeners chose roses and water lilies in synchronizing hues of yellow to unify the space.

Formal Elegance

NORTH ANDOVER, MASSACHUSETTS

Roses, sunken ponds, a grand staircase, and an old stone are key elements in creating a garden space worthy of the most important occasions. The sunken garden at Stevens-Coolidge Place has it all, made even more special by soft shades of pink and an emerald blanket of lawn.

On the Line

NORTH ANDOVER, MASSACHUSETTS

The French Garden is meant to serve two purposes. First it sup-
plies the herb and vegetable needs for the home, and second is
its artistic aspect. Sections of the garden are filled with a variety
of different plants, offering the viewer a juxtaposition of colors
and textures while gazing across the garden, as well as an array
of fragrances while walking through it.

Sunken Living Room

Stevens-Coolidge Place was the summer home of diplomat
John Gardner Coolidge and his wife, Helen Stevens Coolidge.
Originally named Ashdale Farm, it had been in the family since
1729. Now part of the Essex National Heritage Area, its beautiful gardens are open to the public.

Picketing Posies

NEWBURYPORT, MASSACHUSETTS

A pretty window box of annuals compliments the repeating
pattern of the picket fence below. A container of petunias,
strategically placed behind the fence, binds the scene together.
The color scheme can easily be varied with the seasons or for
special events.

Tiptoe to the Water

SALEM, MASSACHUSETTS

The House of the Seven Gables, in Salem, Massachusetts, offers perfect examples of low plantings that maximize and do not obstruct the views beyond the garden. Spring tulip bulbs, when planted *en masse*, reach the same height. This garden's flow of colors draws the eye out to the ocean and to the boats moored in the harbor.

Step-by-Step (top)

MARBLEHEAD, MASSACHUSETTS

The purpose of a perennial border is to create the perfect flow along which to walk. Here, a collection of cascading textures takes us gently to the waters just ahead. The large border stones flow seamlessly along the steps. Soft, fuzzy textures, warm colors, and furls of foliage encourage walkers to pause before heading for a cool dip in the ocean below.

The Right Scale (bottom)

MARBLEHEAD, MASSACHUSETTS

Size matters when adding accents to the garden. The stone bench and birdbath are in perfect proportion to this setting. A larger display of either one could overtake the scene. In this residential garden design by landscape designer Ellen Cool, the use of similar materials for the bath and bench creates a cohesive plan, as does the repetition of annuals along the border.

Stairway to the Sea

MARBLEHEAD, MASSACHUSETTS

The purpose of this brick pathway is to bring guests down to the water. However, along the way, they will enjoy a cheerful mixed border planting. Because this area will be exposed to harsh conditions during the winter, the homeowner has chosen mostly perennials, which will remain safely dormant in the cold months.

Backyard Beauty

MARBLEHEAD, MASSACHUSETTS

A classic mixture of perennials, annuals, conifers and deciduous trees creates a serene scene in this wonderful space. The New Guinea impatiens, with their burgundy leaves, are complemented by the dramatic Japanese maple (*Acer palmatum*). Several conifers, which stay green all year, have been scattered throughout to give winter interest.

Pretty Pitchers *(top)*
SOUTH NATICK, MASSACHUSETTS

The blue heron appears ready to strike at some unseen fish as it stands motionless among the pitcher plants in a private residential water garden. Among New England's most unusual garden perennials, pitcher plants need bog-like growing conditions and a few hours of sunshine daily to maintain their bright green, red, and yellow hues.

Colorful Welcome Mat *(bottom)*
ROCKPORT, MASSACHUSETTS

Climbing vines, low growing alyssum (*Lobularia maritima*) and brilliant annuals shout a loud welcome at the cobblestone entryway of this home. The height of the sunflowers and morning glories on either side of the double-hung windows accent the house from the outside, without restricting the flow of light to the inside of the residence.

Tastefully Done

ROWLEY, MASSACHUSETTS

Limited plantings are perfect for this bungalow-style entry at
Jewel Mill. The homeowner has chosen a pale pink in the plantings and in the wreath to complement the stone wall, and
touches of red to complement the windows and doors. Spider
flower (*Cleome hassleriana*) is an ideal choice for a small space.
Often these annuals will reseed themselves from year to year.

Drop Anchor

ROCKPORT, MASSACHUSETTS

So often, the last item to go into the garden is the thing that makes the greatest impact. Perhaps from a family ship, or perhaps a treasure found at a local antique store, this rustic anchor grounds the garden and adds a special finishing touch.

Rest for the Weary *(top and bottom)*
ROCKPORT, MASSACHUSETTS

All the hard work of gardening deserves a place to enjoy the
fruits of one's labor. A single chair is perfectly situated in this
garden to enjoy the cornucopia of color, and the classical statue
adds a touch of serenity. Such additions to the garden are a
matter of personal preference.

Late Summer Sedum

ROCKPORT, MASSACHUSETTS

As the weather turns cooler, the colors heat up—at least when it comes to this magnificent sedum display. Light pink at first, these smashing succulents sizzle in the late summer sun. Sedums need little care and are adaptable to a wide variety of soils. They make an excellent choice for both seasoned and novice gardeners.

The Lincoln Famliy Home (*above*)

MANCHESTER, VERMONT

Perfectly maintained parterres lead patrons through to the rear postern of this magnificent estate, built by Robert Todd Lincoln in the Georgian Revival style. The simple collection of colors in the formal gardens designed by Lincoln's daughter, Jessie, was intended to resemble Gothic stained glass. In winter, the pattern will flourish despite the bitterness of the season.

Summer Favorites (*opposite*)

NEWBURYPORT, MASSACHUSETTS

Lilies (*Liliaceae*) bring bold color and stature to any garden. In recent years, many gardeners have chosen to forgo growing these summer favorites, which succumb to the whims of the ornamental lily beetle. A strict integrative pest management regime can return these magnificent and reliable bulbs to their rightful place in New England's summer display.

Roundabout Design *(top and bottom)*

WOODSTOCK, VERMONT

The circular design puts a strong emphasis on the focal point in
this scene. The designer has chosen to use a natural material as
the walkway, which helps to ground the very busy plantings
around this fountain at Marsh-Billings-Rockefeller National
Historic Park. Many of the flowers, such as the gladiolas, can
be cut and brought indoors.

Marsh-Billings-Rockefeller National Historic Park

WOODSTOCK, VERMONT

Black-eye Susans (*Rudbeckia hirta*) heat up this garden at summer's close, while the towering meadow rue (*Thalictrum polygamum*), in the background tops out its season with feathery mauve flowers. These sturdy souls can attain heights of 12 feet and rarely need to be staked. Brilliant spotted tiger lilies (*Lilium michiganense*) dot the foreground.

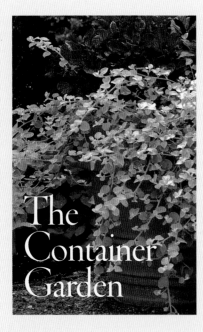

The Container Garden

The only limit to container gardening is one's own imagination. One of the fastest growing segments of the home garden industry, container gardening continues to rise in popularity due to the ease and versatility of growing plants in a small controlled environment. The array of colors and textures available for containers makes them a great way to create a miniature garden, patio or deck without breaking the bank.

Rule of Thumb

OGUNQUIT, MAINE

The appearance of the container may not matter when growing certain trailing annuals. Here, the plants have grown so large that they render the pot incidental. This creates the illusion that the flowers are living in the wall. The strong visual effect of the white birch is softened by the frilliness of the grouping.

How Does It Grow?

OGUNQUIT, MAINE

Specially-blended soils for these self-contained worlds are lighter and hold more moisture than garden soil, and even automatically feed the plants. A large enough container will allow trees and shrubs to thrive in the summer and survive through the winter. When selecting woody ornamentals for containers, choose varieties a full zone colder than ones to be placed in the ground.

Moving Parts *(top)*

BERKSHIRE BOTANICAL GARDEN

Many self-contained plantings, such as these pots of begonia, can be moved if necessary. The pots have aged and have a rustic look. Although there are no blooms, the swirls of color are interesting and brighten a shady corner of the patio.

Anything Goes *(bottom)*

DANVERS, MASSACHUSETTS

A whiskey barrel, an old tire, a hollowed rock or even an antique wheelbarrow can be transformed into a garden. The challenges are to prevent the soil from running out, and to keep the container from rotting. A plastic liner in anything wooden will help prolong the life a favorite planter.

Wall Softener

STANLEY PARK

Imposing walls sometimes can overwhelm a garden. A gardener can use plants to trail over and along a wall to soften the hardscape and make it more inviting. Wall plantings also prevent passersby from sitting on the wall. Either way, the lime potato vine is spectacular.

Expect the Unexpected *(top)*

NORTH HAMPTON, NEW HAMPSHIRE

Along the woodland path at Fuller Gardens, a meticulously restored 1920s mahogany bridge gives a view of the koi pond and leads further into the Japanese garden. The naturally-occurring warm red tones of the woodland floor are mimicked in the bridge. Leaf litter, when allowed to decay, helps to conserve moisture and build humus.

A Little Garden Music *(bottom)*

NORTH HAMPTON, NEW HAMPSHIRE

At approximately one-quarter scale, these happy 19th century figures bring life to the formal garden. Former Massachusetts Governor Alvan P. Fuller purchased *The Cherubs* on one of his many trips overseas. Their small size makes the surrounding garden seem larger; a useful technique to create the illusion of a larger space.

Graceful Respite

NORTH HAMPTON, NEW HAMPSHIRE

In the memorial garden to Lydia Fuller Bottomely is the graceful mid-15th-century Italian sculpture of a woman quenching
her thirst in the reflecting pool. The weathered fence in the
background, softened by lovely conifers and ornamentals,
makes an effective backdrop for the scene.

Wishing You Well (top)

NORTH HAMPTON, NEW HAMPSHIRE

This stone well head, dating back to the turn of the 20th century, no longer is in use, but it makes a terrific garden ornament. Of special note are the climbing black-eyed Susan vine (*Thunbergia alata*) and the crabapple tree (*Malus*) in the background.

Remains of the Day (bottom)

NORTH HAMPTON, NEW HAMPSHIRE

A stone feature, most likely the remains of an 18th century fireplace, is the centerpiece of this perennial garden. When Alvan T. Fuller bought the property in 1920, he left the chimney in place and added this marble-and-lead fountain. The plantings have been left to grow wild, giving the entire area an appropriately rustic feeling.

Survival of the Best

NORTH HAMPTON, NEW HAMPSHIRE

At Fuller Gardens, horticulturists mix several varieties of roses
together in a bed. This use of multiple rose species, each sharing
different disease and insect resistance properties, assures a
healthier garden than one employing a monoculture. While
these roses require more care than any other plant at the gardens, each year brings new and important data.

139

Bring On The Color! *(top and bottom)*
PORTSMOUTH, NEW HAMPSHIRE

Petunias are a must in the annual garden. Reliable, drought-hardy and in love with hot summer weather, they bloom continuously until frost. When paired with like colors and hues, the entire garden says, "WOW!"

Striking Structure

PORTSMOUTH, NEW HAMPSHIRE

A stroll through Prescott Park makes it clear why Josie F. Prescott wanted to share her land with the public. The ten pristine acres stretching along the Piscataqua River have more than 500 varieties of plants. Here, a beautifully constructed brick walkway winds its way past a venerable weeping tree and bold plantings of impatiens.

Day-Brightener

Even on gray, cloudy days, plants in bloom can brighten a
favorite corner of the yard. The larger the plantings, the bigger
the pop of color. Here, two clumps of helianthus hide parts of
the fence, giving it a more natural look.

A Bug's Eye View *(top)*
PORTSMOUTH, NEW HAMPSHIRE

From far away, we often miss the hidden beauty of the garden. Closer inspection of individual flowers, and even parts of flowers, reveals miniscule worlds, each unique unto its own.

Zesty Zinnias *(bottom)*
PORTSMOUTH, NEW HAMPSHIRE

Among the easiest annuals to grow, zinnias make great cut flowers and come in a wide range of colors, textures, and heights. These longtime favorites prefer rich, well drained soil and are a joy to anyone who loves bright, long lasting color. As an added bonus, the bold blooms on these botanicals attract butterflies.

Repeating Forms

Columnar or oval, sleek or bushy, short or tall: each variety of plants has its own unique way of growing. The cascading waterfall at The Fells is complemented on either side by a vine that seems to flow gracefully into the pool. The perfectly placed stingray sculpture mimics the vine's ray-shaped leaves.

Mystery Behind the Door

NEWBURY, NEW HAMPSHIRE

The Fells was the summer retreat for three generations of the Hay family, including Secretary of State John M. Hay, who also served as private secretary to Abraham Lincoln. A very special highlight of this magnificent early 20th century estate is its walled secret garden. Its interesting gate, medallion, and stones give it a fairy tale magic.

Summer Vacation

The boys in this exceptional piece look right at home searching for frogs, salamanders and the bugs of summer. The sculpture is incorporated perfectly into the natural setting. There are no large plantings to obstruct the lifelike scene.

Reading Sentries

Two serious inquirers guard the entrance to the Secret Garden.
Innocence and *Innocence 2* by Lawrence J Nowlan of Vermont
reflect the serenity of the garden. Do not disturb them, for
they are deep in thought. Rather, quietly stroll across the yard,
breathing in the spring air and taking pause at all that is green.

The Great Garden

SUGAR HILL, NEW HAMPSHIRE

No book, course or formal education was involved in creating
this natural setting. It took millions of years to frame the scene,
dominated by purple hills and a valley full of wildflowers.
Simple in form yet bold in stature, it takes the breath away.
Mother Nature watches this garden with a keen eye.

Songbird's Perch
SUGAR HILL, NEW HAMPSHIRE

This hybridized version of lupine is frequently seen on roadsides throughout northern New England. Many believe it to be indigenous to the rugged coast of Maine, but in reality it is not. Though beautiful, this June bloomer is becoming a concern because it crowds out native species of plants.

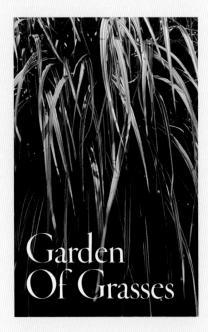

Garden Of Grasses

Very few perennials can be sustained in a New England garden throughout all four seasons. However, a plethora of ornamental grasses serve that purpose well. Whether they are used to fill an entire garden, to create a structured border, or are carefully placed as focal points, ornamental grasses have a place in practically any landscape.

Ornamental grasses are desirable for their movement, shape, color and inflorescence (flowers). In fall, they display flower and subsequent seed heads ranging from *no big deal* to a light-capturing spectacle of movement.

Slice of Serengeti
WICKHAM PARK

Zebra grass (*Miscanthus sinensis 'Zebrinus'*) towers behind a clump of coneflower (*echinacea purpurea*). Grown for their variegated foliage, these thick beauties can achieve heights of up to seven feet.

Vertical Sprays

STANLEY PARK

Grasses are very effective in adding a vertical element to the garden. Much like sculptures, these ornamental favorites can stand alone or in a clump. The sunlight dances through the individual blades and changes each hour. The show is particularly lovely in late afternoon, just before sunset.

A Little Blue Grass *(top)*

COASTAL MAINE BOTANICAL GARDEN

Echinacea and Russian sage give color to this bed of mixed plantings. The striking blue color of Elijah blue fescue, (*Festuca glauca*) pairs well with low-growing junipers that also have hints of blue. In the back right, a stand of switchgrass, (*Panicum virgatum*) has come into flower.

What Fence? *(botom)*

STEVENS-COOLIDGE PLACE

Ever wish that fence in the yard would just disappear? If sunshine beats against the scene all day, it is a perfect spot for a large clump or two of ornamental grasses. Remember to plant them far enough in front of the fence to allow for the plants to mature. Over time, the fence will vanish and yield a less austere look.

Blue Sunshine

DISTINCTIVE GARDEN DESIGNS

A large clump of a hakone grass (*Hakonakloa*) shines brilliantly, surrounded by perennial cornflowers (*Centaurea montana*). The green cornflower leaves look particularly deep against the hakone grass, while the blue flowers and yellow grass play against each other and provide wonderful hues to capture the summer light.

Fire and Water

BOOTHBAY, MAINE

Art can be placed in the most unlikely spots to add impact,
elegance, or a bit of frivolity to the garden scene. *Helios*, a
stunning glass sculpture by Eric Hopkins, was truly the centerpiece of the pond during the 200/ Atmospheres exhibit at
Coastal Maine Botanical Gardens. The sculpture complements
the iris and grasses by mimicking their forms

Something To Eat?

BOOTHBAY, MAINE

Amusing sculptures bring life and added beauty to the Fairy House Village at Coastal Maine Botanical Gardens, one of the largest botanical gardens in New England. Artist Squidge Liljeblad Davis had some fun with these ceramic wolves, part of a temporary exhibit, while a cat and bear sculpture she created are on permanent display.

Weathered Pergolas *(top)*
BOOTHBAY, MAINE

The salt air and sea spray have rendered these structures a wonderful shade of gray that blends perfectly with the stone walkway. Experienced gardeners know that the elements will change the color and texture of almost any landscape structure over time. Once the newness wears away, the patina that remains will be part of the final design.

Sea Glass *(bottom)*
BOOTHBAY, MAINE

The sea green color is not typical of the Maine Coast, but Henry Richardson's *Chiseled Orb* has an oceanic feel. There is sure to be plenty of chatter generated by surprised visitors who stumble upon something so unique in this coastal setting.

Quiet Contemplation

BOOTHBAY, MAINE

Forged from stunningly beautiful pieces of Maine granite, the Vayo Meditation Garden offers Zen-like simplicity at the water's edge. A philosopher might say that reflection and rumination are found growing alongside the majestic pines of this rugged coast.

Sweet Smell of Summer *(top and bottom)*

YORK, MAINE

The star of this fragrant show at the York Harbor Inn is a spectacular collection of ornamental casa blanca lilies (*Lilium 'Casa Blanca'*), flanked by purple morning glory. Pots of perfectly placed petunias catch the eye and draw it upward to the magnificent umbrella palm (*Cyperus alternifolius*), waving in the breeze.

Enter Here

YORK, MAINE

To garden is to create art. The plants—vibrant and muted; bold and soft, dark and light, warm and cool—are the paints we use to create our landscapes. In the beginning, the garden is there to welcome us. When we leave, it is the last thing we see. From the smallest cottages to the largest mansions, our flowers, trees, and shrubs set the tone for the places we live and work.

 **Michael Hubley** is a self-taught photographer who began his study and practice of photography in 1985. His work has been published in five photographic books on New England and a number of magazines, and he has received several prestigious awards at local and national levels. Most of his images were photographed through the lens of Nikon film and digital cameras. Michael dedicates this book to his wife, Alison, for her love and support in all his endeavors, and especially his love of photography. To view more of Michael's photographs, please visit michaelhubley.com or email him at hubley519@comcast.net.

 **David Epstein**, a lifelong resident of New England, was born in Portland, Maine. He received an undergraduate degree in biology from Colby College, and holds a masters degree in counseling/psychology, and an MBA, from Boston College. He received his training in meteorology at Lyndon State College in Vermont and has been an on-air meteorologist for more than 20 years. After working for stations in Connecticut, Maine and Vermont, he joined his current station, WCVB-TV, Channel 5 in Boston. He also teaches meteorology at Framingham State College. David indulges his love for gardens and flowers with his landscape design business, Bloomscapes, Inc. and his Internet garden site, www.GrowingWisdom.com.